CH00840391

Everyday Mindfulness – Change Your Life by Living in the Present
Jennifer Brooks

Copyright 2012 by Empowerment Nation

EmpowermentNation.com

Table of Contents

Introduction: This is Your Mind...
Welcome to It!

Congratulations are in order. Whether this is your first foray into the ancient practice of meditation or the continuation of a journey, you're to be commended. Why? Because it means you've taken that vague "searching feeling" within you and decided to act upon it. You may not know exactly what it is you're searching for. You may not realize exactly why you're plagued with an inexplicable feeling of anxiety – or perhaps even panic. But there is one thing you're very certain of: *You're tired of living this way.*

Undoubtedly, like most of society, you've found yourself hassled, your nerves are jangled, and you feel just plain stressed out. But unlike many, you've made up your mind that you really don't have to live like this anymore. You're looking for a refuge—a sanctuary—even if only for a few moments a day. You're finally searching in all the right places!

Mindfulness Meditation as Part of Your Life

Perhaps you've hesitated to meditate because you're fearful that once you begin, you'll be transformed into that guru sitting on a mountaintop alone. You imagine that your only contact with the outside world would be those intrepid few who climb the treacherous landscape to tap your wisdom. A valid fear? Perhaps a *stereotypical* fear, but definitely not a valid one. The truth of the matter is that you can set aside a mere twenty minutes a day and still become a guru of sorts – minus the mountaintop experience.

Twenty minutes of sitting still, quieting your mind. That's it. According to some scientific studies you can gain phenomenally increased focus in as few as *four short days*. Surprised? It's true! Continue this practice for eight weeks, according to the results of another research report, and the benefits are simply incredible. Mindfulness meditation certainly deserves more than a cursory glance.

Mindfulness in Another Form

For many individuals, even twenty minutes sounds like an interminable length of time. If this is you, then you may want to consider the benefits of informal mindfulness. Instead of sitting still, struggling with those thoughts floating through your mind like the canoes in the Tunnel of Love, focus your mind carefully and deliberately on the daily tasks at hand. You can turn any activity into a meditation session this way, from washing clothes, to booting up your computer, to framing a house.

That's no exaggeration. In this way, you're practically mind-melding the "guru on the mountaintop experience" with your daily working lifestyle. It just doesn't get any better than this. In fact, I believe this is such a beneficial approach to mindfulness that I've devoted an entire chapter to it – including providing you with examples you can use to kick off your mindfulness journey.

The practice of mindfulness can create miracles in your life, if you let it. Not only can it improve your focus and heal you physically, it can transform you into a more compassionate and loving individual. You know the type: *the person everyone loves to be around*. You can be the calm eye in the center of a tornado. You will become the person who others come to for advice as well as words of solace. You'll be able to handle your life in a manner that others will want to emulate.

The bottom line, though, is that you will finally have some sense of what you've been searching for all these years. That vague yearning will be fulfilled. The longing for a better life will vanish, and you'll finally see it lying out before you. Moreover, you'll come to the realization that it was right in front of you all that time. If you have any regret about your journey into the pursuit of mindfulness, it'll be that you wish you would have begun it sooner.

What this Book is All About

By now, you're probably getting excited – or at least hopeful – about mindfulness meditation.

3

While it's certainly no panacea, it is, nonetheless, a very useful method for dealing with the stresses, obstacles, and unexpected events of your life. No one says that during your first few days of meditation, you'll suddenly turn into the Dalai Lama. In fact, you probably won't notice much difference at all. But continue with the practice regularly – preferably daily – and you'll slowly begin to see a difference.

Not only that, but others around you will notice a difference as well. *Guaranteed.* How can I promise you this? Because it happened to me. I once was at a loss at how to handle the issues of my life. I'm not talking just about those huge, overpowering crises that life throws at us; I'm talking about being anxious about every moment of my existence, from what lunch I should choose to what clothes I should wear in the morning. Good grief! I couldn't even decide on what radio station to play in the car.

After years of living this way, I could take it no more – and neither could my friends or family. I approached a good friend who seemed to have his life pulled together. If he worried, he never showed it— no equivocations on small, inconsequential decisions like lunch or a radio station. He chose bravely. But more than that, he had a quiet aura around him. He radiated compassion and love. I decided I wanted to be more like that—and thanks to the methods described in this book, I've succeeded.

Consider this book your knapsack on your journey to mindfulness. What can you expect to find in this little book of wisdom?

- An explanation of what mindfulness really is. And *isn't*.
- What a beginner's mind is, and why it's actually quite important.
- What role your breath plays in calming your mind.
- Tips for taming your wandering mind.
- How enhanced attention to your body can help you cruise along your journey with ease.
- The difference between formal and informal meditation, and how to put these practices to work for you.
- The healing power of mindfulness.
- A variety of techniques – both informal and formal – to help you develop a lifetime practice.

Start Today. Right Now, Even.

Why waste another moment of your life suffering from stress, indecision, or experiencing that foggy feeling that there has got to be more to life? Instead, start your trek to discovering how sweet, rich and fulfilling life can really be.

Read this book over once. Then use it as your reference as you develop your own program of mindfulness. Does formal meditative practice work better than informal practice? Are some activities more conducive to performing informal mindfulness? Make a note any time you're experiencing an especially satisfying mindful moment. Then try to repeat it.

At first you may not be able to. At first, you may even think that the one moment of pure mindfulness was a fluke – that this incredibly rich feeling will never choose you again. But stay with it. You'll soon discover these moments come with greater ease as you travel down the road.

You're entering an entirely new phase of life. Savor every moment of it.

Chapter 1: Get Off that Fence and Experience the Moment: Mindfulness Explained

Are you a fence straddler? Imagine yourself climbing a fence. You swing one leg over the top. You plop yourself onto it so that one leg is on one side of the fence and your second leg is on the other. Given enough time you'll eventually move so you're on one side of that fence or the other. I'm not psychic in this prediction. There are two good reasons for it. First, the pain isn't worth that seat anymore. Sitting as you are, it's bound to hurt after a while. Second, you've finally realized you're not fully inside the enclosure nor are you fully outside of it.

Many of us—myself included—find ourselves being fence straddlers when it comes to the issue of time. We sit straddling with one leg on the inside of the enclosure, called "the past," and the other on the outside of the enclosure which is "the future." But now, observe where your body is: squarely atop the fence, which is the present.

You're a fence straddler every time your mind wanders into the past or every time it starts dwelling on the future. We all do this occasionally. You may replay an event in the past in order to learn a lesson. Or you may be planning your goals for your future greatness. If, however, you find yourself consistently wallowing in regrets of the past or spending excessive time constructing the perfect future . . .

well, that just isn't healthy. Sooner or later, you'll realize how much it hurts to sit in that position. You're missing the best part of life, the fence. The fence is what's sustaining you. It's the impetus propelling you into the future.

How many times have you failed to fully take advantage of the present moment? How many times do you find your mind wandering to the past or micromanaging the future? Every day, far too many of us lose precious moments of joy and happiness because of the way our minds are positioned in time. You may lose irreplaceable moments with those you love because you're not fully in the present when you're with them.

That's a shame because the present is all you have. *"Yeah, yeah."* You've heard that before. But do you know why? Because it's true. *Very, very true.* So what does all this have to do with mindfulness? Everything. Mindfulness meditation teaches us the joy, advantages, and the necessity of living in the moment.

What is Mindfulness, Anyway?

The practice of mindfulness comes to the West through the Eastern Buddhist spiritual tradition. That, though, doesn't mean you have to become Buddhist or even spiritual in order to take advantage of its marvelous benefits.

The Buddhists would use the term "awakening" to refer to the awareness of what is around you. A second aspect of mindfulness, which many individuals find themselves naturally led to, is the examination of their lives in general. You may find that you're questioning your world view or discovering a growing appreciation for the fullness of the moment.

In practicing mindfulness meditation, you may discover that your newfound awakening has you living all your moments with an extra touch of awareness. Colors may become more vibrant, actions become more meaningful, and opportunities appear to open up where once there were none! The alternative? To continue to live as a fence straddler, not fully appreciative of the very moment in which you're living.

Right now, you may not realize it, but many of your actions are driven by unconscious fears and perhaps even some deep, unrecognized insecurity about the present moment. Perhaps you already notice some of the attributes of one whose life seems to be dictated in these essentially unhealthy ways. You may have lost confidence in yourself and find yourself unable to make plans for the goals and dreams you once considered important. Or you may feel "out of touch" with those around you as well as your environment and your daily routine.

Take Charge of Your Life

It may be difficult for you to believe that mindfulness can turn all of this around. Simple, applied attention to the moment doesn't seem as if it should have this large of a beneficial consequence connected to it, does it? However, if you've already danced briefly with this practice, you may have found small changes that you liked. Perhaps that's the reason you're searching for a more serious or extended practice.

In the final analysis, mindfulness meditation can – if you allow it to – actually change the relationship you have with yourself. After all, you can't change anything outside of you until you begin to alter yourself and your fundamental views of your environment and the world at large. This sounds a little grandiose, granted. Right about now you're probably saying, *"I just wanted to meditate to reduce stress."* You've certainly come to the right meditation bench for that. Without a doubt.

What are the changes you may experience with this amazingly simple approach to life? Jon Kabat-Zinn, in his book, ***Wherever You Go, There You Are***, explains that you'll develop the "art of conscious living." It's that simple. Sit quietly for twenty minutes a day and change your view of yourself and the world. Sure, you can do that. This is the ultimate case in which the appearance is deceiving. Simple, yes. Easy? Well, I'll let you decide.

If you're ready to meditate – and believe me, it must be a decision you come to after some, well, *meditation* about it – then you should prepare yourself for the time, effort and discipline which accompanies this achievement. You also need to know that, yes, you may feel incredibly different in just a few short days. Your focus can be sharper in as a little as four days, scientific studies tell us. You also need to practice it for a longer period to fully appreciate all the possible changes.

A Habit to Last a Lifetime

The goal becomes this: once you start meditating, you'll create a lifelong habit. Mindfulness meditation can take you, moment by moment, into an increased awareness that can not only transform the way you approach your life, but can also transform your very health.

Why should it be so "difficult" to change your outlook? For one thing, you've probably been viewing the world in this way since childhood. Your point of view is, moreover, likely due to experiences you've had along the way. You see things the way you do, because your mind says you have an excellent reason to. In other words, your unconscious mind is justifying your view. An unconscious mind is a stubborn creation; just trying to reason with it can be akin to wrestling with a crocodile. You're not going to find it easy – at least not at first. But that doesn't mean it's not worth the effort.

I'm confident you'll find the mere attempt at mindfulness to be immensely satisfying. You'll be amazed at the many facets of your life it puts you in touch with. Perhaps some of these you once were intimately connected to. Others, though, you may never have known you possessed. In either case, you're sure to find yourself changing – so slowly at first you barely notice the difference. If you do notice it, you may chalk it up to other reasons. When you realize your joy is more intense, you're feeling a sense of peace you've seldom experienced, or you have a deeper connection to your family, you may still not connect it to your mindfulness practice.

A Note on Meditation

So far, we've talked about the mindfulness aspect of meditation, but we haven't spent much time preparing you for the meditation portion of this aspect. For many, myself included, this is sometimes equally as difficult as keeping your mind in the present moment. You must try to keep your normally active body sitting or lying still. This again goes against the grain of not only what your mind thinks, but what society thinks as well.

As you sit there, you simply observe the tiny moments of present. The catch is that you don't change your thinking through judgment. Instead, you become the outside observer. You're encouraged to ask such questions as "What is happening?", and

"How do I feel about it?" Ask yourself what you see. Question what it is you hear.

In many ways, as you sit there, apparently doing nothing, your mind will be on heightened alert. You're using all your senses to fully absorb what is going on around you. And you're doing this with a stillness within your body that may feel quite foreign to you. You're not concerned with hustling from one end of the office to another, about getting the clothes in the washer in time for soccer practice, or typing furiously to meet your supervisor's deadline (or perhaps your own self-imposed deadline).

Another Kind of Mindfulness

You'll also discover that you can perform each of these duties described above with a mindful consciousness. This is what is referred to as an "informal mindfulness," and it's been practiced by many for thousands of years. You may be most familiar with it as used by Brother Lawrence, a Carmelite monk of the seventeenth century. Brother Lawrence approached every activity – even washing dishes in the kitchen – with an acute awareness of the present. As a consequence, those who knew him said he was enveloped in a sense of peace unattainable to most individuals. Brother Lawrence's peace was contagious—so contagious, in fact, that those closest to him wanted to know his "secret." He related a continuing and often detailed description of practicing "the presence," as he called it.

You continue your normal routine throughout the day, but you bring your mind to bear on every moment of your actions. While this may seem like a trivial, even a futile, exercise, you'll be utterly astounded at the potential for a substantial transformation.

Mindfulness is an aspect of life far too many of us overlook—even purposely push aside. Perhaps you find it too painful to live in the present moment. It could be that you're too busy counting your regrets in your past. Or it could be you're doing the classic American number: excusing your lack of present moment awareness because "life got in the way." From this moment on, you'll find yourself conscious of every moment as you straddle that fence of time. Soon, you'll discover how uncomfortable you've been all these years.

Chapter 2: How Mindfulness Heals

You're seriously considering taking a giant leap into mindfulness meditation, but it's all a bit frightening to you. After all, you're entering new terrain here. You're not quite sure what you may find. The fear of the unknown is strong. Now take that fear and combine it with your comfort zone trying to persuade you that your world is perfectly fine just the way it is. Yes, I certainly can understand your hesitancy.

Seven Reasons to Practice Mindfulness

In addition to achieving a heightened awareness of the moment, there are many reasons to practice mindfulness meditation. These reasons can easily be described in two fashions: the *long* and the *short* explanations. I've listed seven of most beneficial *short* ones below.

1. Quiet preparation.

What does this mean? Many individuals have credited mindfulness meditation with the healing of mind or body, or the boosting of creativity in their work. In actuality, meditation slows you down for the needed amount of time to allow you to find the creativity that has been hiding inside you all along. Similarly, mindfulness can help you listen to your body in order to recognize that healing is actually needed. Once you can see this, then you can direct your body in the proper direction.

2. Getting to know you.

This may sound corny. Though they may sound like questions from the Hippie Generation, these really are legitimate questions to ask: "Who am I?" "What am I like?" Stop for a moment to consider these. If the only ways in which you can define yourself are through your social and familial roles, you may not know yourself as well as you think.

Mindfulness meditation can help you get back in touch with what many call the "authentic you." With your newfound sense of the present, you'll be more aware of your thoughts and feelings. You can't help but get to know yourself better.

3. Improves your sex life.

Now, some of you may think this isn't a benefit of much importance. Then there's that small group of you that know how vital a good sex life is to your overall health and happiness. This advantage is one which is especially beneficial to women, who seem to be more judgmental of themselves in the bedroom than men. Acquiring the ability to live in the moment helps to quell the judgmental self-talk that females often go through while they're making love.

4. Side-stepping mental traps.

There's a popular saying that asks, "What's the definition of insanity?" The answer: "Doing the same thing over and over and expecting different results."

That may not be insanity, but it is definitely a type of mental trap. One pitfall of a mental trap or mental stagnation is finding it difficult to problem-solve. Think of the greater potential that each day could hold if you could spend less time problem-solving. Imagine if you could analyze the situation faster and then come to a decisive decision – one you knew in your heart was right. If you could do this, you then would confidently go on to the next issue without the need of straddling that fence of time. Indeed, you'd be far more productive.

5. Quelling the monkey mind.

Never heard the term "monkey mind?" This is the term for that endless influx of thoughts which float through your brain all day long. It's especially apparent when you attempt to clear your mind, as in when you sit down to meditate.

In reality, you listen to your monkey mind all day long. We all do. Roughly guessing, you'd be right in saying the vast majority of these thoughts are negative. "What made you think you could even qualify for that promotion?" "Who are you to start your own business?"

Mindfulness helps to subdue the negative feral chatter in your head. Again, this chatter is nothing more than your mind trying to drag you back to the past or have you actively worrying about the future. When you spend more time in the moment, you spend less time obsessing about either the past or the future.

6. Welcome to the world of calmness.

You've just been cut off by a driver on the road. How do you react? Do you immediately give him some sign language or yell at him, even though he can't hear you (and wouldn't care even if he could)? Perhaps you allow the incident to irritate you for the next 28 miles.

If you answered yes to any or all of those questions, you may be in need of mindfulness meditation "therapy." If the Dalai Lama drove, what would he do in the same situation? He would probably conduct himself with a little more dignity and quite a bit more serenity. He might even go so far as to send the thoughts of loving kindness and compassion to the driver who cut him off.

You may never reach the level of a Dalai Lama or achieve the supreme state of calmness he exudes. But once you begin your meditation, your road rage will certainly subside. You'll also notice you react more calmly in other situations as well.

7. **Increase focus.**

Did you ever see the movie "Up?" In it, there's a talking dog (yes, you read that correctly!) with a limited attention span. He'll be in the middle of a conversation when a squirrel catches his eye. His mind completely leaves the conversation as his eyes follow the movement of the small animal. He announces, "Squirrel!"

How often do you find yourself in this position, either in conversation or while you're working on an important deadline? Mindfulness meditation won't stop you from seeing the squirrels in your life, but it certainly can help you from blurting their presence out when you're in the middle of something else.

Meditation Benefits All Ages

You're never too old to start. That should be the tag line for mindfulness meditation. Certainly if I were to make a commercial recommending this practice to the public, I'd use it. Why? Because it's the truth. The truth, by the way, is nothing less than amazing.

You may be thinking right about now, "I've gone through some 50 plus years of life without the need to meditate. Why in the world would I even think about starting now?" What you say is true. You have survived for all these decades. But that's not the same thing as "thriving." Whether you realize it or not, there are special challenges which affect persons as they age. One of these is loneliness.

As you continue in your life experiences, you may find that natural changes are producing a sense of loneliness in you. Have your children moved out and started lives of their own? Gone off to college temporarily? Or perhaps you've recently been widowed. The point is that at this age, life is changing for those around you. They're moving on. You're still at home. Sometimes alone.

According to the research, mindfulness meditation can help you deal with this, especially if you're between the ages of 55 and 85. If you're this age and beginning to feel the twinge of loneliness, why not start a regular meditation program? It only takes two and a half hours of mindfulness a week to experience this lifting of loneliness. This news comes to us from a new study recently published in the professional journal, ***Brain, Behavior and Immunity***. After only two months of mindfulness meditation, researchers discovered that individuals reported feeling less lonely.

While that in itself is a psychological advantage, the physiological benefits associated with this are pretty amazing as well. Just read about what the lead researcher, J. David Creswell, said about it: "We always tell people to quit smoking for health reasons, but rarely do we think about loneliness in the same way." The medical community isn't sure why meditation helps, but it does know that "loneliness is a major risk factor for health problems and mortality in older adults."

Meditation and the Common Cold

"I'm not lonely," you say, "but I am prone to colds and the flu every winter. But I don't think meditation can help me with this. Can it?" Don't be too sure about that. If you suffer from yearly colds like clockwork, try following this advice: Take a vitamin C tablet and twenty minutes of meditation. According to a small study – involving 149 persons – a meditation routine reduced the chances of their acquiring respiratory infections like colds and the flu.

The results of this study were nothing less than impressive. Meditating actually reduced the incidence of infection between 40 and 50 percent. In and of itself, that's a remarkable statistic, but then compare this to the effectiveness of the conventional flu vaccine. The vaccine reduces the incidence of infection by 50 to 60 percent.

If those statistics don't raise an eyebrow, then consider this: Each year approximately 36,000 deaths are attributed to the flu. Additionally, at least half a million persons are hospitalized because of it. The common cold, moreover, causes 40 million lost work and school days yearly. Imagine improving your odds of all of this simply by sitting and living in the present for twenty minutes a day.

Meditation Between Math and Science

Surprised? Many individuals are quite taken aback upon learning that mindfulness meditation is becoming increasingly more popular in schools. Given escalating incidents of behavioral problems and increased conflicts among students, some teachers have turned to meditation simply out of a sense of frustration.

Much to their surprise, these teachers saw improvement in the students nearly immediately. It really should have startled no one, given the results of recent studies of the effects of meditation on children. What scientists refer to as "executive functioning" improved tremendously. Specifically, self-control and self-awareness among seven and eight-year-old students increased. Attention spans also increased in elementary school students, thanks to practicing this regularly.

But more than that, anxiety levels and stress were also reduced, especially among those seven and eight-year-olds. Additionally, physiological improvements were noted in older students. Those students between the ages of 16 and 18 experienced through mindfulness meditation, a decrease in their blood pressure levels. Mindfulness meditation produced better behavior in the students as well as a lessening of aggressiveness.

Mindfulness and ADHD

Part of the reason for the success of this practice in schools may very well be because of the beneficial effects meditation has upon those children with ADHD (Attention Deficit Hyperactivity Disorder). Meditation appears to work especially well on adolescents, according to the *Journal of Attention Disorder*. In one study, adolescents, as well as adults with ADHD, completed training sessions for this specific style of meditation. More than 78 percent of those that completed the sessions self-reported feeling fewer symptoms during this period.

As good as this seems, the news gets even better. Compare this therapy to the standard conventional practice of prescription drugs. Meditation has no adverse side effects. The practice, moreover, is widely embraced by those with the disorder. It also decreases the number of persons reporting depression and anxiety. *Now we're talking really good news!*

In the next chapter, you're going to learn the first step of mindfulness meditation: developing a beginner's mind. It's a concept that will carry you far in your meditation practice – and throughout all your daily activities as well.

Chapter 3: Seeing the World Again for the First Time: The Beginner's Mind

"Of course I have a beginner's mind," you may say. "I'm new at this. It's the only thing I *can* have. Once I get the hang of this mindfulness meditation, I'm sure I won't have that beginner's mind anymore." If this is your idea of a "beginner's mind," you're going to be quite surprised to discover exactly what it really is.

A beginner's mind is really *not* how you start off your meditation work. It's more about how you "end up" in your meditation practice. Now you're looking a little more than confused. Perhaps this quote from Zen teacher Shunryu Suzuki, in his book *Zen Mind, Beginner's Mind*, will help to clarify: "In the beginner's mind there are many possibilities, in the expert's mind there are few."

Briefly, a beginner's mind is all about *attitude*. You learn to open your mind to all the possibilities that the world holds for you, your goals, and your life. No possibility, in the beginner's mind, is "off limits." Your thoughts of "what is" and "what could be," in effect, are unlimited.

When you approach life with an attitude of openness, throwing off all your "shoulds," then you have achieved a beginner's mind. What are "shoulds?" They are the ideas of what life "should" be like—of what you "should" be doing. Very often

25

we pick these "shoulds" up as we travel the path of life; they more than likely come from others telling us how life "should be" lived. We accept their ideas – and society's ideas – of living as our own. It's easy enough to do. But that doesn't mean you "should" do this or that, just because someone tells you so.

Another Look at Beginner's Mind

Another view of the beginner's mind, which falls in line nicely with Suzuki's description, comes from Saadat A. Khan, a Middle East ruler from the 18th century. He says that a beginner's mind "embodies the highest emotional qualities such as enthusiasm, creativity, zeal and optimism." If you truly believe that limits don't exist and that you're capable of doing anything you can conceive, you can't help but approach life with the enthusiasm and creativity that Khan speaks of.

Now you're beginning to get the idea that the beginner's mind isn't as easy as it sounds. In fact, you now understand why it takes some time to actually cultivate it. As you do so, keep in mind that there may be many who'll try to block your progress. Some of these people are well-intentioned. They don't really mean to hinder your progress at seeking an unlimited view of the world. They may never understand exactly what you're aiming for. Let's face it: in your initial stages, *you* won't be sure of what you're aiming for. But the longer you practice mindfulness meditation, the more you'll understand the concept.

It's Easier to Use Analogies . . .

Sometimes, it's easier to use analogies to talk about beginner's mind. As you might guess, Zen teachings are filled with such examples. Don't let the idea of Zen dissuade you from reading these. You certainly don't need any spiritual training or inclination to learn from these classic illustrations. Here are just a few of them:

Empty Your Cup

A celebrated and esteemed university professor paid a visit to an equally celebrated and esteemed Zen master. "I would like to learn the Zen teachings," the professor said. The master served the professor tea. He proceeded to pour tea into the cup of his guest until it was filled to the brim, then he continued to pour.

The professor watched for a short time, then said, "It's filled sir. In fact, it's more than filled. You can't get any more into it." The Zen master calmly stopped then smiled slyly at the professor. "I mean you no disrespect, professor," he said, politely, "but your mind is much like this cup. You cannot learn the basic Zen teachings unless you first empty your cup."

The Elephant in the Room

Six blind men were introduced to an elephant. Each man stood at a different spot around the large animal. Each was then told to touch and inspect the portion they were introduced to. Then they were told to describe their impression of what an elephant is.

The first man walked into the side of the elephant. He immediately said that an elephant is much like a large, hard wall. The second gentleman approached the elephant from the front. His only impression of the creature was of its tusks. The tusks, the man said, were smooth and very sharp. His first impression was that an elephant was much like a spear.

The third man touched the animal's trunk. It squirmed in his hands and because of this he surmised an elephant must be very similar to a snake. The following man touched the beast's knee. "Why, this animal is just like a tree trunk!" he exclaimed. Again, another man touched the elephant, but he felt the ear. "All of you are wrong," he told the others, 'this animal is like a fan."

The final man grabbed the tail and compared an elephant to a rope. These men continued to argue about the essence of an elephant for a long time. It's only when you're open to the present that you can begin to compare an elephant to all these other items. What types of elephants do you have in your life that you need to view from a different perspective?

Here's Why a Beginner's Mind is Vital

You may believe that you're fine with your "expert's mind." After all, didn't you strive all your life to become competent – even working to excel – in your field? Didn't you work hard to discover exactly what was needed to become the best parent possible? Now, you're thinking, "You want me to chuck it all and start all over again? You want me to question everything I've done in the past?"

No. That's not at all what it's all about. It's more about developing an awareness of everything around you. Here's just one example of this inner awareness that may be of vital importance to you:

You're walking down the street late at night. You want to use the alleyway as a short-cut, which you've used a thousand times during the day. However, you've been practicing your mindfulness meditation regularly in the last month, slowly cultivating what you hope is a beginner's mind.

Something – *you're not quite sure what to call it* – tells you it would be better to skip the shortcut and stay out of the alley altogether. You're about to walk into the dark, narrow corridor, when you decide that intuitive voice inside you just might be right. You feel compelled to listen to it. Instead of stepping completely into that alley, you turn around to take the traditional route home.

The following morning you read in the paper that a person was attacked in that alley at nearly the same time you would have been walking through it. That person could have been you. Perhaps there is something to this beginner's mind.

Driving Out the Monkey Mind

Remember the "monkey mind" we discussed in Chapter 2? It's the endless chatter and incessant flow of thoughts that engulf our minds. You've no doubt already encountered it during your meditations, but what you may not realize is that "monkey mind" follows us wherever we go. For example, the monkey mind is present when you're trying to focus on a project at work but find yourself straying to other thoughts. This situation also occurs when you're driving. You're so used to driving and usually take the same routes every day that the "monkey mind" feels it's the perfect time to start talking about any number of things.

The problem comes in when these thoughts disrupt your driving and you fail to pay full attention to either the other vehicles or the traffic control signals. So how can you compete with it? Actually, it may be easier than you think. Start training yourself to look for new things on your trip. Sure, you may have traveled this route hundreds of times, but look specifically for something you hadn't noticed before. See if this doesn't slow that chatter down and help you pay more attention to your driving.

It's not a bad idea to teach your children to do the same thing on their walk to school, especially if you're not walking with them. Not only will they enjoy this "game," they'll also be training their minds to become more aware of any hidden dangers—any strangers or other potentially unusual or dangerous situations.

Getting Serious About a Beginner's Mind

So how do you develop this beginner's mind? Of course, going into a mindfulness meditative state is a start. But your mind is a stubborn thing. Because of this, you may want to adopt a few of these suggestions on cultivating the openness from which a new highly honed awareness comes.

1. Take one step at a time.

That's all you can do. Take one step at a time – in your life, in your job and with your relationships. You can't predict the future and it's useless to worry about the past. So just take that step and enjoy it. Experience the step for what it is: something new and exciting.

As you step, do so gingerly and be sure to experience every small moment that step affords you. It may be a newly bloomed flower, so stop to smell it (Yes even if it is a bad cliché, it's still a great idea!).

31

2. Place the importance of the journey aside.

In that single step you take, learn to delight in it and also to put the vital necessity of the journey itself aside. You'll get to wherever it is you're traveling. By enjoying each and every step of the journey, you'll find it a much more pleasant experience. But more than that, you'll also find it's a much shorter journey than you ever thought possible.

3. Fall down three times, get up four times.

Okay, that doesn't mean the fourth time you fall down you don't need to get up. You know exactly what this is saying. It doesn't matter how many times in the past you may have "fallen down" in your attempts to do something. In fact, it really doesn't matter how many times you may fall down in the future. The only thing that really matters is that you get yourself up again and continue to move forward.

I'm going to tell you to go one glorious step further, in fact. Anyone can celebrate the moments they pick themselves up, but consider also celebrating those moments you fall down. After all, each time you trip up you get closer to your chosen destination.

4. **Keep your focus on the questions, not on the answers.**

This is, after all, the central concept on a beginner's mind. Stop believing you have the answers to everything. Perhaps the question has more than one answer—or perhaps you've been answering the question wrong all this time.

5. **Think only of your actions. Don't pay attention to those who may be watching.**

This may be the hardest suggestion of all to implement. How often do you begin to do something, but hesitate because your mother is watching, your spouse has her eye on you, or your boss is sitting across the room? Forget all of that! Follow this wonderful tip: *Dance as if no one were watching.*

Dismiss all the eyes that are observing you – and possibly waiting to criticize you. What do they know? If they want to be critical of you that badly, they'll even pass judgment when you do nothing. So, keep your awareness only on your actions. Don't worry about pleasing – or displeasing – others. After all, it's your life, your journey, your happiness.

6. **Cultivate the "don't know" mind.**

We've talked about this before, but it certainly bears repeating. Empty your mind much like the tea cup we discussed earlier in the chapter. Tell yourself you don't know – even if it's something you think you may have known all your life.

Once you can truly admit that you don't know – or there may be answers to questions that you've never fully explored, then you know you're on the path to discovering wisdom. As you develop the beginner's mind, you'll discover an entirely new and exciting life, one you never knew existed before. And that's a good thing.

This isn't the end of mindfulness meditation—not by a long shot. In the next chapter, we'll discuss the importance of breath.

Chapter 4: Take a Deep Breath: The Importance of Breath in Mindfulness

Mindfulness is the gateway through which you discover your true nature. While you're doing this, you will inevitably learn about the nature of everything else around you. As part of this knowledge, you'll also learn how to let those tightly held preconceived ideas, beliefs and myths to dissolve. That's why it's so essential that you learn exactly what a beginner's mind is and why you need to approach your meditative session with this state of mind.

All of us live within concepts; we label objects and even thoughts. If you've never realized this before, just look around you. Perhaps you're sitting at a table right now. If someone asked you what a table was, you'd no doubt describe its physical appearance in quite of bit of detail. You may also explain what it's used for. This is your "concept' of a table. Many meditation experts believe that in order to achieve a beginner's mind you must first "stop your mind," so to speak. It's at this point you'll be truly awake to the present moment.

There's no doubt about it, breathing is a physical sign of your life. You can't deny that without your continued breathing you wouldn't be here right now. So it's little wonder that metaphysically and symbolically speaking, breath represents life and continued growth.

Ancient cultures worldwide equated breath with a "life force" – however they described it – which gave life to all things. This is easy enough to see when you delve into the roots of the word itself. In Latin, it's called *spiritus*, which you recognize immediately as the origins of the English word "spirit." In the Greek language the word is *anima*. Notice that this is closely related to our word "animated." The Hebrew word for breath is *rauch,* while *Brahman* is the Sanskrit word.

They all sound different, but they all have similar meanings. These words not only mean "breath," but they all double as the meaning for "spirit" or "soul." Consider what you're ultimately doing when you bring awareness to bear on your breath. First, you're bringing your body and mind into harmony. This alone gives you a sense of peace of mind and contentment. Additionally, it provides you with a wonderful sense of wholeness.

Exploring Your Breath

What's to *explore* you may ask? The only way to get to know your breath is to through careful observation. Later in this chapter, you'll be instructed to count your breaths and to use your breath as a stepping stone to help you experience a deeper mindfulness session. But before you can do that, you really need to know how your breath reacts while it's being observed. And yes, it does act differently. As you purposefully watch your breath, you may actually wonder if you really know how to breathe.

For many, the moment they begin to focus awareness on their breath, two things happen: First, the body tenses up. Then their breathing – affected by this tense state – becomes unnaturally shallow and labored. If this happens to you, it may be that you feel as if you've actually forgotten how to breathe. That's silly. (But you'll find your mind going there!) You've been doing it all your life without giving it any thought until this very moment. Or perhaps you're feeling as if you're somehow breathing *wrong*. Another less than logical thought, isn't it? Because then you realize you're still alive, so you must be doing something right. The truth of the matter is that you may have to adjust your breath slightly while you're watching it.

It's best to begin your observation of your breath by simply "exploring" your breathing. You don't need to count your breaths or try to direct either the breath or your thoughts toward them. Instead, what you're going to do is to become aware of what happens when you breathe. Pay attention to the physical movements of your body. Feel how your rib cage moves up and down. Notice how the rest of your body reacts as well. Even feel the breath as it flows in and out of your nostrils.

Spend five or ten minutes doing this. Then decide what you've discovered that you really didn't know before. Perhaps you've never noticed the feeling of breath through your nose, or how your entire body may be moving when you breathe. Seriously consider how one breath differs from the other. If you're like me, you may have thought every breath would have been identical – the same length, the same depth. Once you feel comfortable with this exploration expedition, then you can move on with confidence to the more formal exercises to develop mindfulness meditation.

Cultivating Mindfulness of Breath

Now we will begin to develop your mindfulness of breath. Everything else flows from this, including an increased sense of concentration. How is this accomplished? All you really need to do to initiate this process is to notice your breath. You can start right now, even though you're not in a meditative session. Notice the rise and fall of your abdomen while you're breathing. Don't judge it if it's shallow or deep, or right or wrong. It just is. This is similar to what you've just done, but now you're initial hesitancy is gone. Your body no longer fears your watchful eye.

Place your hand on your abdomen. In this way you have a physical reminder of the movement of your breath. Place all your attention on the individual breaths. Don't think about the breath prior to this current one. Don't think about the next breath. This is the start. Once you're able to notice your breath, you should track these breaths simply by counting them. For our purposes, a breath includes both an inhale (the rising of the abdomen) and an exhale (the falling of the abdomen).

You can perform this with your hand on your abdomen if you like. Your goal is to breathe 10 complete breaths without losing focus. Yes, it does seem quite easy. Trust me, though—it's more of a challenge than you think.

The widely recommended trick is to recite the word "in" each time you inhale followed by the number of breath it is. You would begin by saying, "In, one" as you inhale. On the exhalation you say "Out, one." Count from one up to ten. Once you've completed this sequence without getting distracted and losing your count, then you count downward in the same manner. Should you get distracted and lose count (and you'll be amazed how often your mind strays), simply start over at one. Don't at any time get irritated by this. Don't judge yourself when this happens. Be gentle with yourself. You know your concentration has improved when you can count to twenty breaths without distraction.

This breath routine is the perfect warm-up exercise not only for mindfulness, but for any style of meditation. You'll also find it exceedingly useful whether you're a novice or if you've been meditating for 25 years. Once you've mastered these first twenty breaths, you're ready for the second step of the exercise. This is to eliminate the external counting.

Simply acknowledge your breaths by saying "in" and "out" during the appropriate movements.

Congratulations! You're well on your way to the road to awareness.

Just When You thought Your Breath Work was Done . . .

That's right! You're well on your way but not quite there – not yet, at least. You still have another vital aspect of breathing you'll want to practice in order to help you become fully aware to mindfulness and to use your beginner's mind to its fullest. You're now aware of your breathing. You now have dropped the counting. The next step is to begin to shed your preconceived notions about, well, *everything* – including your breath.

Don't even think this challenge will be beyond your ability. After all, you've just completed the initial breath concentration exercises. You're more than ready for this. Your goal is to take your awareness of your breath to a new level. In addition to merely being mindful of breathing, you're to ask yourself some searching questions like:" Who am I?" and "What is this?" The latter question can be asked in regard to anything and everything. Remember, you're entering mindfulness with an open mind, void of preconceived ideas.

Practicing this exercise involves more than being aware of your breathing and throwing questions into the air – even though that may be what it sounds like at the moment. Imagine that you don't know what inhaling your breath actually is. Now, physically inhale and be aware of only that portion of the breath in that short moment. As you complete the inhalation movement and it turns into an exhalation, you'll notice a momentary "gap." This occurs when the inhalation stops and right before you exhale. Focus on this gap next – even in the short time it occurs. As you exhale you're then to be aware of that portion of the breathing process as well. Remember that throughout all of this you aren't supposed to know what breathing is.

It may very well be that your initial reaction is one of fear. You may become frightened when you begin questioning the foundation of your knowledge. After all, if you approach breathing without knowing what it is, then how can you really know anything? At the same time you'll probably discover it's also one of the most liberating experiences of your life. Why? Because you have a fresh perspective of everything as well as the freedom that accompanies the shrugging off of those assumptions.

Chapter 5: A Love Affair with the Present: Taming Your Thoughts

"If your mind isn't clouded by unnecessary things, this moment is the best moment of your life." How I wish I could claim I said that. A Zen master, though, spoke those wise words. *Prepare yourself for a love affair with the present moment.* If you live your life on that fence we discussed earlier, with one leg dangling in the past and the other anticipating the future, you're about to learn how to remain seated in the present. By the way, it really is going to be the best ride of your life.

You'll learn to love your new perspective, but before long, you'll wonder why you stayed straddled – and strapped – between these "time zones" for so long. When you experience more of the amazing powers of focus and concentration, you'll see that the ability to calm your mind is an added benefit. You'll also be able to avoid what you now believe are unavoidable bouts of agitation. But that's really only the tip of the iceberg.

The longer you practice this form of meditation, you'll discover your thoughts deepen. It's almost as if a curtain will be lifted so you can view the origins and meanings of those thoughts. They'll no longer be nagging you, but you'll be able to analyze them in order to deal with them more effectively. Those unpleasant, even painful feelings—the ones that have been building up--will suddenly burst into the air and you'll no longer be burdened by them. Once you're able to penetrate that heretofore impenetrable fortress, you'll gain exciting crystal clear insight about matters important to you.

When Do You Start? You Already Have!

I can see you now, ready to get started. You're no doubt tired of regretting the things in the past you can't change, words you can't take back, or actions you can't undo. You're tired of pining for a future which may never occur or one that may actually materialize filled with the fears you're feeding into right now.

So where do you start? Believe it or not, you already have. You have, at least, if you've attempted even one of those breath exercises in the previous chapter. For those few moments in which you focused solely on one small breath, you've tasted what will soon become a love affair with the present. This ability to focus on the present – or as you've experienced so far, your breath – is referred to as a "one-pointed focus." As you achieve ever-increasing success in this one-pointedness, you'll discover that distractions quickly fade into the background.

It may be that you're in a crowded coffee shop trying to read your favorite novel. Prior to your mindfulness practice, you probably spent more time listening to the conversations of the diners at the other tables. Sure, it *looked* as if you were reading, but you really only read a page or two. Even then you had to go back and go over it a second time to ensure you really understood what was happening. You were paying more attention to the conversations and individuals around you than to your book.

After even as short a time as a month of mindfulness training, you'll notice that no matter how crowded the coffee shop becomes, you're better able to keep your mind from straying. You're busy reading that book. All the noises seem to fade into the background and the words on the page take center stage.

Now if these were the only good reasons to meditate, it would definitely be good enough. Your thinking can be more productive at work if you weren't distracted by your co-workers' personal phone conversations or other noises. How awesome would it be if you could filter those background noises so that they don't interfere with your personal serenity and focus?

Your Relationship with the Present Moment

How often can you say you live fully in the present moment? If you're like most of us, *not often enough*. Why? After all, living in the present appears to most of us to be a utopia. What more could you ask for? In reality, though, it's a frightening place. When you decide to live in the present, then you have to face all the baggage the present brings with it. This could mean different things to different people.

When you live in the "here and now," you can't hide from the baggage by excusing yourself with regrets over the past. You can't run from it by trying to chase the future. Far too many of us have created a gigantic maze of thoughts simply to avoid living breath by breath. Some individuals construct these wonderfully sound houses of suffering and pain. Many meditation experts call this their "narrative." A narrative is nothing more than a story. These people, for whatever reason, have made suffering and pain their story. In many ways, it may even define them.

Why would anyone do this? Perhaps you already know the answer. If they continue the "pain dialogue" they don't need to admit that there's a chance they might be happy. Others only want to see the happiness; they want no part of acknowledging any pain they may have locked inside them – either physical or emotional. If they do recognize it there, then in the present moment they may have to confront it.

What's Your Story?

If you dare to live in the present moment – and trust me, it certainly is worth the effort – then you have to admit to yourself that you've been hiding portions of your emotions for a while. You may be saying, "Not me! I don't have anything to hide." But are you sure?

Think about the last time a potentially negative thought appeared. Let's say you identified it as "terror," whether it originated from a physical or an emotional source. What was the first act you took? Did you live with it – that is, face it in the present moment? Or did you create a veil of thoughts to place in front of it so you could pretend it wasn't there? Did you make excuses about why you were feeling this terror, or did you simply push it back behind the curtain by busying yourself with distractions of social events, shopping or television shows?

From this perspective your mind is totally amazing. As Andrew Weiss said in his book, **Beginning Mindfulness,** your mind is "prolific." Indeed it is. It can – and does – create endless distractions to drag us out of the present. Your mind never tires in re-creating the story of your life – from its own special perspective – from the past well into the future. There's only one problem with this: It prefers to skip over the present much like a pebble skipping over a placid lake. It chooses *which scenes* to recreate.

Coming to Rest with the Present

Your task is to stop your mind from hopscotching through the story of your life, regardless of the emotions which may surface. Sure,

46

you may discover you're harboring some deep suffering you haven't pulled out of the closet in years. But what if you learn, by minding the moment, that you have a well-spring of joy inside you, waiting to burst forth? Which would be harder to accept?

The Present is no Golden Ticket

Remember in the movie *Willy Wonka and the Chocolate Factory* the rush to find one of the five Golden Tickets in a candy bar? These tickets would admit the holder into the inner sanctum of the chocolate factory. It seemed at least on the surface like a dream come true. If you recall the story, though, merely having that golden ticket didn't change a thing in anyone's life. If they were dissatisfied, grumpy or mean before, that's exactly how they viewed the chocolate factory. It was only Charlie, who entered the chocolate kingdom with a sense of wonder, hope and possibility, who exited in the same way.

The present moment is a lot like that chocolate factory. Simply stepping your foot through the door doesn't guarantee that your suffering will magically be gone—that your fear of joy will vanish, or even that you will find peace of mind. What it does, though, is to make you aware of the scenario your mind is constantly playing on your behalf. So what do you do to tame these out-of-control thoughts? The first step in acquiring a state of mindfulness – of calmness and serenity – is to

47

confront it. It may be that much of your anxiety is lifted just by acknowledging it.

But more than that, you must recognize your need to approach the present from a consciousness of trust. You have to trust the present to be the perfect moment that leads you where you ultimately need to be. Without this trust, you won't find freedom from anxiety or fear—or even of regrets of the past. Without this trust, you'll continue to view the future with anxiety, convinced it's ready to ambush you at any time.

Don't Blame Your Mind!

You may be reading this now and pointing blame at your mind. *If only* it didn't constantly create the story of your life. *If only* it could just leave you alone long enough so you can enjoy a sliver of the present. Only then would you truly understand who you really are, what you're actually doing, and even what you *should* be doing with your life. Instead, it insists on continuing this "monkey chatter."

Stop. Don't blame your mind. You can't "blame" your mind for thinking anymore than you can "blame" your heart for beating. After all, your mind is tasked with the responsibility of thinking. Your mind is performing the job it was created to do.

Many novice mindfulness students use the phrase that they're "caught up in their thinking."

Excuse me? Exactly what does that mean? It means that these individuals are attached on a very personal level to the narrative the mind is playing out for them. "Why, of course, I'm attached to it," you may say. "After all, it's my life. I do take it personally."

Your attachment to these past and future thoughts accomplishes only one thing: They keep you believing you're powerless. *Powerless in changing your thoughts. Powerless in your approach to your relationships.* In effect, you may have come to believe you're impotent to everything about your life. In a nutshell, the story your mind has created and recited back to you over again like a well-loved bedtime story is nothing more than the rationalization of your emotions.

Your mind, therefore, holds another power over you – and for most of us it's a big one. It's the creation of your habits. Your mind does an excellent job of hiding your power to change your habits.

Stop My Mind, I Want to Get Off!

If it's the job of your mind to think, then how can you possibly help it to think so it's actually benefiting you? This may sound a bit counter-intuitive, but you first must develop and cultivate an appreciation of your mind. I don't mean an appreciation of just the portion that can effortlessly perform a flurry of math problems in record time. I'm not talking about the extraordinary grasp of physics or languages it has.

Your mind, believe it or not, doesn't necessarily "see" everything. Before I go any further, allow me to use two examples to aid your understanding. Think of the classic dog whistle. You blow it to call your dog home. When it whistles, though, you don't hear a thing. Every dog in the neighborhood hears it and responds by barking. Your ears obviously don't hear everything. The same is true with your eyes. Every day when you walk outside and soak in the sun, ultraviolet rays are hitting your skin. Can you see them as they bounce off your body? No, but if you receive too many of those rays, you'll find them the following day in the form of a golden suntan – or maybe even sunburn.

So it is with the present moment. It contains more – *much* more – than you are aware of. The point of this brings us back to the beginner's mind. Once you realize there are things you certainly haven't thought about and questions that you never knew to ask, you realize your mind really doesn't "see" everything. In this way, you detach yourself in yet another encore presentation of your mind's version of your life. You take those tentative, even frightening, first steps out of your comfort zone. And to think – this journey started with the power of the first breath on which you focused.

Chapter 6: Paying Attention to Your Body

You've come a long way since you first started exploring the idea of mindfulness meditation. While you're not completely finished with your learning journey, you've made incredible progress in putting all the pieces of the puzzle together. The process of being mindful isn't a topic easily described; it's best understood when it's experienced. You've only touched on this experience. Trust me, it gets even better.

In previous chapters, you've become mindful of your breath. I hope you find this a useful tool whenever you're feeling stressed or tense. Merely taking a few breaths and keeping yourself perfectly focused on them can make a tremendous difference in how you approach the bumps you encounter along the road.

Now you're ready to turn your mindfulness toward your body. It's not really as difficult as you may be imagining. Remember how you were mindful of your breath? Put your hand on your abdomen. Feel your abdomen moving up and down, rising and falling with every breath you take. Guess what? That's a very simple way of being mindful of your body. All you do next is expand this awareness to other areas of your body.

Mindful of Your Body

Mindfulness of your body is an excellent habit to develop – and you'll discover you'll be using it in some form whether you're formally meditating or not. At the end of this chapter, you'll be introduced to a simple technique that relaxes your entire body.

As with any form of meditation, you'll become aware of sensations of various parts of the body. One of the exercises you're exposed to is one of being aware of your hands. Being aware doesn't mean judging their appearance. It doesn't mean diagnosing the fact you think you have some symptom of some disease. It means you're merely noticing – in great detail – your hands. You're not to make any comments like, "I must be developing arthritis in my fingers."

Your job is not to evaluate whether the particular body part is painful. Of course you'll notice the pain. But that's all you're to do: simply notice it as one of the many attributes of this body part. You simply take note of the sensations and the feelings and record them in your mind that they exist. Judging your sensations does you absolutely no good. Besides, it's contrary to everything mindfulness is.

Here's a quick example to illustrate exactly what I mean. Hold up your hand. Either one, it makes no difference. Look at it as if you've never seen a hand before. Describe it. What color is the skin? Is it an even color tone on every part of your hand? Do you see any scars? How about wrinkles? Don't judge the presence of any of this; merely observe all of this, as if you were viewing someone else's hand.

Now examine the palm of your hand. Describe it. Look at the lines where the joints of your fingers are located. Scrutinize the lines on your palms. Notice the color of your palm. Take notice of every detail regardless of how small or trivial it may be. Don't hurry through this experience. Become a witness to your hand. *No judgment. No analysis. Merely observation.* If you discover a scar, don't allow the mind to start telling you the narrative of how silly you were to allow the incident to occur which eventually formed the scar.

Examining with Your Eyes Closed

That's the first part of the experience. Now that you've completed it, you can continue onto the second part. This portion involves you closing your eyes. Read the directions below. Then, with your eyes closed, perform this.

Raise your hand, but this time keep your eyes closed. Allow your wrist to move the hand. How you move it is totally up to you. You may also choose to curl your fingers and then straighten them. Place your attention – but don't touch the fingers – on the thumb, then the forefinger and all the other fingers, one by one. Don't hurry through this. Take your time.

Place your attention on the palm of your hand—all while keeping your eyes closed.

When you have completed this awareness experiment to your satisfaction, open your eyes. Was this non-visual placing of attention on your hands different from actually seeing your hand? In mindfulness meditation, this second experience is referred to as "the felt sense of the body." It's a non-conceptual experience. Its value lies within the experience itself.

Now that you have an idea of experiencing awareness of your body, here's a valuable exercise to become aware of your entire body. Not only that, but by performing this exercise, you'll also be relaxing your body. It's not an experience you'll soon forget or one you'll perform once and never do again. It has the potential to become a valuable tool to help you relax on a regular basis.

In comparison to the ancient origins of mindfulness meditation, this exercise is really a baby. It's about thirty years old and is roughly based on Jon Kabat-Zinn's original body scan. The purpose for which Kabat-Zinn created it was for stress reduction—and it certainly serves its purpose in that department. But for your purpose right now, it's the perfect method of becoming aware of your body. This exercise alone may take fifteen to twenty minutes in order to perform correctly. There's no need to rush through it. In fact, you receive much more out of it when you take your time.

Being Mindful of Your Body

1. **Make sure you're wearing comfortable clothing.**

   If it all possible, change into loose-fitting clothing. If you can't do this, simply loosen the clothing you're currently wearing. If you have a tie on, loosen the knot some. Unbuckle your belt.

2. **Find a comfortable location to lie down.**

   That's right. There's no other option but to be on your back. You may want to retrieve your yoga mat and lie on this. You may even want to borrow a comforter from your bedroom, place it on the floor, and use this.

3. **Place your hands at your sides.**

   Make sure your legs are slightly apart.

4. **Become aware of your body as a complete entity.**

   Be especially aware of those places in which it's making contact with the floor.

5. **Close your eyes.**

6. **Focus on your feet.**

Move your feet and toes as you wish. The goal, in addition to being aware of your body, is to relax the body as well.

7. Release all of the tension from the feet.

Simply allow them to "melt away" into the floor.

8. Bring all your awareness to the parts of your legs – your shins, calves, thighs, and hips.

Imagine both of your legs becoming unusually heavy. Then you feel them as being extremely relaxed. Imagine your legs melting slowly into the floor.

9. You now focus your attention to your lower abdomen.

This should be a bit easier. You're already accustomed to focusing on your abdomen for your breathing exercises. There's one difference, though. Instead of merely observing your breathing, you're to visualize your lower abdomen as totally relaxed. Imagine any tension you may have in this area simply slipping away. At the same time, you're taking deeper breaths.

10. **Shift your awareness to your upper abdomen as well as your chest, neck, and throat.**

Feel these areas getting heavy, then relaxed. After that, they'll feel as if they melt into the floor.

11. **Direct your awareness to your shoulders, your arms (both upper and lower arms), and your hands.**

They, too, become heavy and very relaxed, and then seem to melt into the floor.

12. **Place your awareness on your face and your head.**

As you relax this area, feel the tensions simply fade away. The head, too, will feel as if it's simply melting into the floor.

13. **Now that you've completed relaxing every area of your body individually, scan your entire body.**

In this step, you're double checking to ensure there are no areas you may have skipped over that still feel tense or stressed. Should you discover some, just go through the same procedure to relax them.

14. **Feel your body being totally relaxed, with no edges and without any identifiable parts.**

15. **Stay in this relaxed position for ten minutes if you can**.

   At the very least, try to remain like this for five minutes.

16. **Wiggle your toes slowly.**

   This indicates to your body that you're emerging from your cocoon of relaxation.

17. **Next, slowly wiggle your fingers and stretch your arms and legs.**

18. **Open your eyes.**

19. **Gradually sit up.**

20. **Now's the time to review exactly how you feel.**

   Are you feeling more relaxed than when you started? Does your body feel lighter? Do you see the world any differently?

   Now you're well on your way to developing a mindfulness of your body. You know what it feels like to be aware of the various parts of your body.

You also know how to examine your body without judging it in any way.

Chapter 7: Formal Mindfulness Practice: No Tuxedo Necessary

Formal mindfulness doesn't mean you need to wear a tuxedo to your meditation session. It's merely the term coined to describe the awareness you experience while you're in a meditation session. The other term you'll hear used is *informal mindfulness.* This refers to the awareness you bring to bear on your daily activity. Don't think of it as a choice, though. Eventually, there'll be no choosing between the formal and informal. Once you start experiencing the benefits of mindfulness you'll want it to flow to all parts of your life.

In fact, many meditation experts will tell you the ultimate goal of sitting with mindfulness is to be able to take that wonderful feeling along with you wherever you go and bring it to whatever you do. It's a fundamental truth that one of the aims of mindfulness is to be able to navigate the ups and downs of your life. As you progress in this, you'll learn to be less "reactive" and judgmental to events and more accepting.

Within this formal mindfulness practice, you have several options from which to choose. Of course, you can meditate while sitting. At the appendix of the book, you'll find the directions for this common session. But, there are several other effective approaches to mindfulness which don't require you to remain in the classic sitting pose.

Formal mindfulness can be experienced through lying down and meditating, movement meditation, as well as walking, to name just the most common approaches.

Are You Going to take This Lying Down?

Well, are you? You certainly could – and you'd be all that more mindful because of it. If you've already attempted the body scan in the previous chapter, then you have a good idea of what formal mindfulness meditation is like. It may be that as you explore your options this becomes your preferred choice.

Of course, as with any formal session, you want to ensure you wear comfortable non-constricting clothing. There's nothing worse than settling into a much-anticipated session only to find your jeans are too tight or your shirt feels a little snug. While you don't need to buy special meditation clothes, you do need to carefully choose what you wear. It's also best if you grab your yoga mat from the closet and use this to lie on. No, yoga mat? No problem. Retrieve a comforter or a blanket from the bedroom—or simply borrow the afghan from the back of the couch for now.

Wait! Don't get down on the floor just yet. You'll also want to find a firm pillow to support your head and neck. If you don't think you have one that's quite firm enough, try placing a book underneath it. It may take you a few tries to find a book of just the right size. Your initial reaction may be to lie with your legs flat. That's fine if it's not painful or uncomfortable. It's not, however, absolutely necessary. If you feel the least bit of discomfort, find a second blanket, roll it up and place it under your knees. Your feet should be placed flat on the floor. You'll discover this to be much better for your back. Now you are all set to meditate. Simply use the directions in the appendix.

Walk It!

"Walking? How could I possibly meditate as I walk? Are you sure about this? I've been known to have trouble walking and chewing gum." Relax. A walking meditation is quite simple, but it does require your constant attention. This is truly a challenge to your ability to be mindful and not so much to your ability to walk.

Normally, you use walking as a mode of transportation. This seems obvious. You walk, essentially, to get from Point A to Point B. Much like breathing, the vast majority of us take it for granted. It's something we do automatically, with no thought to how it all happens. Have you ever really been truly aware of the sensations involved in this activity? If you're like most of us, you probably haven't. You'll be surprised to learn the moment you actively shift your attention to becoming mindful of these small and easily overlooked movements, you'll open up a

62

whole new world. You'll understand why so many individuals choose this approach.

The First Step? No Step at All!

Ready to take your first step? Would it surprise you to learn that it's really no step at all? This may sound like a Zen koan, but remember, it's all about adjusting your state of mind. Your attitude is everything. Your first task is to simply notice the sensations of your body while you're standing still. You'll eventually use these observations for the baseline of your meditative session. Remember that you judge nothing. You merely observe and mentally record.

Your task is to scrutinize the many barely perceptible movements your body goes through just to stand motionless. Go ahead. Give it a try. Stand up now. You're about to discover that standing without moving requires a myriad of very small movements. Then you'll use these observations as your baseline for the observations you'll find yourself making during your mindful practice.

Start your "standing motionless" examination by observing your feet. Make a mental record of how your feet feel. As you focus your thoughts on your feet, relax the muscles. Notice the difference in feeling from being in a tense state to a relaxed one. Really take note of this. Far too often many of us hold portions of our bodies hostage, keeping them in a tensed state without even realizing it. Perhaps we do this because we've never been able to distinguish the difference between what the muscles feel like in the two different states. Simply observe, almost as if you're watching a movie.

What you've just done with your feet, repeat with all your other body parts. If your thoughts should stray – as they likely will – simply and gently bring your mind back to your body. You don't need to chastise yourself for this. Sweep the thought away and be done with it. There are at least two ways to deal with these stray thoughts. Some individuals actually say "thank you" to the thoughts before they escort them out of their minds. Others simply silently say "next." This signals the mind to drop the thought and refocus on the meditation.

Once you've escorted the thought out of your mind, calmly return to observing your body. This exercise initiates a dynamic shift in the level of your awareness. As you scan every part of your body, it places you in the proper frame of mind to perfect the physical movement involved in this deliberate form of walking. It also enables you to recognize the act of self-realization involved in this activity. A walking meditation is an excellent method of "letting go," or releasing your concerns and worries so that you can finally appreciate the moment.

Can I Walk Yet?

Just when you think you're prepared to start the actual walking portion of this meditation, I'm going to stop you one more time. This time I'm providing you with a suggestion. It's all about your chin. The level at which you hold your chin, believe it or not, provides very accurate insight into your mental state. Those who walk with their chins lowered, eyes directed toward the ground, are usually experiencing negative emotions. Those at the other end of the spectrum – those who hold their heads upward – are normally absorbed in thoughts outside of the world.

You probably know where this is heading. Neither of these types of individuals is placing their focus where they should be: squarely in the present. So where should your chin be pointed? You're absolutely right! *Parallel with the ground.* You should not be looking down, or looking up. Instead, keep your glance straight ahead; your chin will follow. And your thoughts will naturally remain in the present moment.

Before You Take Your First Step!

"What? I'm not ready to take a step yet?" No, but you're definitely getting closer. Trust me, you're really close. Many individuals call this form of mindfulness "deliberate walking." As you perform this, you'll take notice of your movements, just as

you did when you were standing still. One of the acts you'll be using is "labeling." This has nothing to do with identifying something and placing judgment on it. It means you're identifying your movement and naming it. *Period.*

Your first several forays into deliberate walking will be in a simple straight line. The only time you will make a turn in your walk is when you turn around to go in the other direction. Choose a starting point as well as a realistic ending point. Don't make it too long of a trek, especially in the beginning. You may get discouraged.

Follow the instructions below. Yes, now you're ready.

1. Stand

We've discussed this: The observations you acquire here become your "baseline" for the sensations to come.

2. Before you take a step, label it, "intending to walk."

3. Take your initial step.

Lift your right foot, slowly. Then, just as slowly, place it on the ground. While I've just described this in what seems to be two separate motions, you perform this as one fluid – slow – motion. Label this as "placing."

4. **Don't move for one or two moments.**

5. **Lift your left foot.**

   Make the same fluid movement you did with your right foot. As you place the foot on the ground, label this as "placing."

6. **Pause again.**

   Don't move for another moment or two. Once you reach your destination, place your feet together.

7. **Continue in this manner, including the essential one or two-moment pause between steps.**

8. **Once you reach your destination, place your feet together.**

   Mentally label this as "pause."

9. **Slowly shift your awareness.**

   Label your non-movement as "standing." (Pretty clever, isn't it?)

10. **Now you'll prepare to turn and walk in the opposite direction.**

    Before taking any step toward this goal, label this moment as "intending to turn."

11. **Start with your right foot, and lift your toes.**

Pivot your heel and turn to the right. Mentally, label this as "turning." The heel, by the way, stays firmly on the ground. Your head is aligned with your torso. Meanwhile, your left foot, as you probably have already surmised, remains firmly on the ground.

12. **Lift your left foot.**

This foot doesn't pivot. Place it next to your right one. Label this movement as "turning." You're now standing in the opposite direction.

13. **Pause.**

14. **Repeat the steps of walking as outlined above until you reach the point at which you originally began.**

Moving Meditation

Yes, it is true that meditation – especially formal meditation – involves sitting or lying still. But we've seen that walking can be an especially productive form of mindfulness as well. Moving meditation comes in handy on two levels. First, if you feel you absolutely can't sit still any longer or you

68

can't lie without moving your muscles, you can use this technique. It helps you to adjust your body into a more comfortable pose without losing that relaxing, introspective attitude.

This approach can also be used as a form of meditation in itself as you sit or lie. In fact, you may want to practice this a bit before you attempt any informal approach to mindfulness. The theory behind this is easy – and I do mean *easy*. Let's say you're sitting in a meditative session, when you get the sudden urge to move your foot. You need to readjust it, but the last thing you really want to do is to break the state you're in. So, instead of just quickly moving the foot, you first think about it and label what you're about to do as "moving the foot." Then very slowly you adjust your foot. This could be done in any way you choose. The key is that you do it slowly.

Mindful Eating?

Really? Yes. If you've never heard of this before, let alone tried it, you're about to change the way you approach food. Mindful eating is nothing less than feeding your body with all the awareness of the elements and effort needed to make your meal a reality. In a smaller scope of awareness, you'll also discover the true taste and flavor of your food. When you eat in this manner, it will be a benefit not only to your attitude, but to your health as well.

You may find this whole approach to mindful eating a bit foreign. That's understandable. It is for many of us. To prove this to yourself, start your excursion to mindful eating with a quick trip to the closest fast-food restaurant to you. It really makes no difference what restaurant it is. I'm not even asking you to eat anything.

Sit in the dining area and watch others eat. Now, without judging anyone, answer this question: Is anyone eating slowly? According to what little you already know about mindful eating so far, how many persons do you see practicing it? If your answer is few to none, don't be surprised. It's called fast food because you receive it quickly after ordering it. But it can also be labeled this due to the speed at which many eat it!

If you give it some thought, it can be a sad commentary on our society's lifestyle. Now, think back to the times you may have been caught up in this frantic race to clear your plate. Perhaps you take quick lunches between important meetings. You realize afterward you really didn't even taste your meal, you ate it so fast. Or it could be you grab a quick supper after work so you're not late in taking your child to soccer practice or ballet class. If you can relate to either of these examples, or add your own, then you can definitely benefit from a session or two of mindful eating.

Mindful eating is a form of meditation that's much easier to show exactly what it's all about than to tell you. You can perform the following exercise with any type of food you wish. My introduction to mindful eating was through a small unassuming raisin. You may think this isn't much of an exercise. But I have a confession to make. Prior to this exercise, I hated raisins–everything about them. I couldn't stand their taste or texture. When I actually paused long enough to reflect on what I was eating, though, it tasted vastly different than what I had eaten before.

In this exercise, you're about to use an orange, but you can use any fruit you'd care to. What you're about to experience is the best-testing food you've ever eaten – guaranteed.

1. **Place an entire, unpeeled orange on a plate in front of you.**

2. **Imagine you've never seen an orange before.**

3. **Scrutinize the orange – everything about it. Use all of your senses. Breathe in the aroma, feel the skin, look at the color.**

4. **Peel the orange.**

    This is where you're really going to notice the texture of the fruit.

5. **Contrast the texture of the meat of the fruit itself with the peel. Be sure to notice the weight of the fruit as well.**

6. **Pull the wedges apart.**

   Feel the individual slices. Don't judge them, simply experience them.

7. **Take your first bite.**

   Yes, finally, you can take a bite. As you do so, note the flesh of the orange and the juice as it floods your mouth. Perform all of this as slowly as possible.

8. **Thoroughly chew the bite of orange.**

   Yes, this is probably the same advice your mother gave you when you were younger. She was right all along. Not only chew the bite of orange slowly and thoroughly, but stay aware of all the sensations involved in the process.

   That's it! Now sit back and reflect on the process. Was that not an extraordinary eating experience? How did the taste of the orange differ from other oranges you've eaten?

Mindfulness to the Meal

This is just a small sample of the potential mindful eating has in your life and on your health. You're about to learn how to put this technique to work. You're going to sit down to a full meal. Remember, you can do this using any meal you wish. Hopefully, you'll eventually extend it to nearly every meal.

1. **Before you start eating, take a few moments to be grateful for the food.**

   This may take any form you like, from saying grace to sitting quietly in silence over it for a moment.

2. **Place your awareness to the hand with which you eat.**

   Do this even before you take a first bite. In some ways, this is an effective way to center yourself.

3. **Take your first bite.**

   You don't want to take a big bite. Your goal is to realize the taste, texture and other sensations of this particular food. If you've performed the "orange-eating" exercise, then you know exactly what's involved in this initial bite.

4. Resist the mind's need to judge the meal.

Oh, you know that it'll try. Your mind immediately may say, "Way too hot!" It may decide it lacked the proper seasonings. Or perhaps it's trying to tell you the taste is a big disappointment. This is not to imply that you're to ignore these reactions. Simply note them and dismiss them politely.

5. If you can't sit in silence during the meal, then take note of how the conversation affects your eating.

Ideally, many say you shouldn't talk during a mindful eating session. Of course, that's the ultimate situation. But if you're trying to put this technique into effect regularly there may be times you'll be required to talk. That's fine. Just be mindful of this as part of the process as well.

Mindful eating is a great experience any time, but it's especially helpful if you're performing a day-long or half-day of meditation in your home. You can continue your mindfulness even while you're eating. The more often you can eat mindfully, the more you'll enjoy your food. But more than that, you'll discover a new calmness washing across you.

Chapter 8: Reaching Into Everyday Life: Informal Mindfulness

If you've been able to experience that mindful state we've been discussing for even a few moments in formal meditation, then you know the exquisite gift it is. You may already have begun an earnest quest for it, sitting in what you hope is a state mindful enough that you can capture the feeling. *Non-judgment. Just essence.*

In those few moments, you have discovered your true self. Sit back for just a moment. What if you could experience that as you conducted your daily activities? Why is it a gift that's saved for those precious meditative sessions? How would your life be changed if you could experience the core awareness of yourself throughout the day?

Before you dismiss the idea, recall our brief discussion on a concept referred to as *informal mindfulness*. This is bringing your mind to that heightened state of awareness which you acquired in meditation—but instead of merely sitting in this state, you're carrying it into your daily activities. You can bring informal mindfulness to actions as diverse as washing clothes, swinging a hammer, or placing the key into the ignition of your car. In doing so, you'll begin the most incredible journey of all: Living in the present moment.

From there, it's only a matter of time before you discover an entirely new understanding of yourself and the world around you. You can't do this, though, without first slowly introducing informal mindfulness into your daily habits. Don't expect to jump in, performing every action in a mindful state. Few individuals have ever done this even after years of practice. But you can start out by choosing just one activity.

It is also essential that you familiarize yourself with all the preceding exercises, and learn about mindfulness in a meditative setting. All the preparation you've done in this book up to now has brought you to this one moment: where you can imbue your daily activities with mindfulness.

No, It Doesn't Magically Appear

Don't think you're going to wake up one morning to discover that every action you make is magically enhanced with this awareness. If it really did happen this way, most of us wouldn't treasure the experience as much as we do. Your aim is to start slowly. Most students select one activity initially. Perhaps it's something as common as driving your car. To begin, in fact, it could be an activity as narrow as driving your car to work in the morning. This would be useful on several levels.

First, it ensures that you perform this activity close to the same time every day in order to create a discipline. It's also a grand opportunity to bring some inner awareness to what for many is a very stress-filled event – depending on the traffic and your view of your job. *Stop-and-go traffic. A speed limit sign that's teasing you. The anticipated run-in with your supervisor should you be late.*

Exactly how do you bring some mindfulness to this insanity? Start even before you place the key into the ignition. Sit in the driver's seat and take several deep breaths. Become aware of your breathing, just as you would in a meditative session. Next, slowly place the key into the ignition. Listen to the engine start. Become aware of everything involved in driving – from your hands on the steering wheel to your foot on the accelerator and brake pedals. Even notice your weight against the seat.

Even more than any of these observations, it's essential that you notice your reactions and thoughts as you drive. Bring a heightened awareness to the traffic patterns around you—the way the cars travel and at what speed. Are there specific cars that are acting erratically? Pay particular attention to your reaction to various situations. Did some driver just cut you off? As you begin to react with anger, instead take several deep breaths. Also, take note of what music or talk show you're listening to as you drive. How does this affect your feelings?

Even though these observations shouldn't be made in a judgmental fashion, they serve to truly educate you in how your feelings translate into actions during what many consider a stressful event. This very well could be the start of eliminating that stress and filling the space with serenity.

The Ubiquitous Cell Phone

Is there any greater opportunity than to start your informal program by choosing the ringtone of your cell phone as a call to mindfulness? Just as monks use bells as indicators of periods of awareness, your cell phone is the perfect tool for this discipline. This may be especially productive when you hear the tone for a text or an email notification. Neither of these requires an immediate "Pavlov's dog" response from you.

Instead of instinctively reaching for the phone without thinking, use the sound as a chance to draw several deep breaths. Use this as a time for centering. Once you're centered, read the message. How do you react to the message? Examine your feelings or even lack of feelings. Do this as often as you can throughout the day. If you'd like to, extend this practice into your telephone conversations.

When you're engaged in conversation, you can figuratively stand back and listen to it as an "observer" of your own actions. What emotions are you experiencing as you talk? Is it annoyance, impatience or anger? Is it joy, pleasure, happiness? Perhaps you're responding calmly to the person on the line but seething on the inside. Become aware of this as well. Again, though, don't judge yourself. Just watch yourself play this scenario out.

Even though cell phones are considered by many as the bane of our existence and a glaring symbol of everything wrong with our society, you can turn this into an invaluable tool for self-realization.

A Little Mindful Exercise, Anyone?

Exercise – yes, the physical type – and mindfulness just seem to naturally go together. This is, without a doubt, an outstanding opportunity to shift your awareness. Regardless of your exercise routine, make a conscious effort to move beyond merely "thinking" throughout your exercise routine to examining the movements of your body. This is especially useful because, by its very nature, physical exercise offers repetition of movement.

Your awareness can start with following your breath. From there, you can mindfully examine the sensations of your body as you jog, use the treadmill, or even lift weights. When you discover your mind is trying to decide on the dinner menu or – worse yet – the type of sundae it wants after the workout, bring it back to your breath. From there you can notice the feelings of your body again.

If you do this for any length of time, several things are sure to occur. First, you'll be more engaged in your exercise program. You may even look forward to it more now. Secondly, you may notice that this time is vastly more productive than it ever was before. By staying aware of your body, you'll be performing the exercises with more precision. This could very well translate into better health and quicker, healthier weight loss.

Oh, No! Not the Computer!

More individuals than ever before spend their entire work day tethered to their computer. Perhaps in no other area is it easier to lose awareness of your body. This means that bringing a spirit and awareness while working is vital. What if you were able to sit at the computer and become absorbed in the sensations of your body – at least at regular intervals throughout the day? Perhaps you wouldn't end your day quite so tired, drained, numbed, and with your eyes so glazed over.

Devise some method to use as a signal that upon hearing it you'll pause. If you receive audio notification of email delivery, use this as a reason to pause. If you don't have such a notification, merely set the alarm on your cell phone to alert you several times throughout the day. During this short period, take several mindful breaths, feeling the rise and fall of your abdomen. Notice your sitting posture. It's probably less than perfect. But don't judge. Merely note it and by all means correct it. Perhaps your body is tense. Certainly, as you become aware of any tensions, correct them without scolding yourself to get into that position.

Household Chores

Really? Yes. Right here, in a variety of ordinary – dare I say boring? – tasks throughout the day, you have a grand opportunity to experience awareness. Even something as mundane as loading the dishwasher, folding clothes, or sweeping the floor can be used to garner mindfulness. When you enter into any of these chores with the expressed intention of being mindful of your body, something magical happens. The act which you once did out of duty or necessity becomes an almost sacred experience.

Notice every physical aspect of the activity. If you're sweeping the floor, examine how your arms propel the broom. Are you loading a dishwasher or washing the dishes by hand? Notice how the water feels on your hands. Scrutinize how your hands feel as they move in order to put the soap on the plates, rinse them off, and finally place them on the dish drainer or hand dry them.

You can also use cooking as a mindful experience. The results become even more spectacular – not only for you, but for your family as well. The awareness you pour into cooking actually changes the way the food tastes. You may scoff at this, but don't be too smug until you actually try it for yourself. As you bake a casserole, imbue yourself with an awareness of your body, of the texture of the food and all aspects of the activity. If you don't think you can do this throughout the entire preparatory session, then choose one aspect. As you continue, bring your mind back to your breath as you remember. Even a small effort brings large benefits.

These are only a few ordinary activities which have the potential to be transformed into extraordinary events with just a small effort. As you go about your day, you're sure to discover even more routines that are personal to you which can be filled with a mindful presence.

Informal mindfulness has the potential to create a seismic shift in your life. But don't expect to be able to make this change in your life immediately. Just as you worked your way through following your breath, becoming aware of your body, and other aspects of mindful meditation, you'll need to work up to a conscious awareness of informal mindfulness. The good news is that it can be achieved.

Chapter 9: Sprinkling Seeds of Mindfulness: Daily Tips

"All this information is great," you say, "but by the end of the day, I realize I've gone through the entire day doing fewer informal mindfulness exercises than I had originally planned. Heck, sometimes I even make excuses for not sitting in a mindful state for twenty minutes. Is there anything I can do to get kick-started?"

We all have that complaint at one time or another. Here are ten tips that you can easily slip into your day without even realizing you're doing it.

1. Stop Multi-Tasking

What? How can anyone possibly survive the day without multi-tasking? Sometimes, it's the only thing that keeps individuals from drowning in a sea of chores at work and at home. Or so we believe.

For the most part, we all do some form of multiple jobs at some point in the day. Perhaps you talk on the telephone and load the dishwasher. Instead of trying to do three things at one time, slow down. Perform only one. If you're answering your email, do just that. If you're searching for a particular item on the web, perform only that search.

If you're frying a meal, don't run out of the room when some brilliant idea to do something else strikes you. *One thing at a time*. Then, once you can conquer this, perform that one task slowly, deliberately, and with mindfulness. This isn't the easiest tip to follow, but you'll discover that it just may be one of the most valuable.

2. Become More Aware of Your Surroundings

This doesn't just mean to become a "people watcher." Rather, it is a suggestion that you become more aware of all of the small things around you. The wall hangings, the mug you're drinking out of, or even the hairstyle of someone you love.

How many times have you walked into a room, seen something you thought was new and asked, "How long has that been there?" Then you're embarrassed by the answer, "For about a month." It's been there all that time, but you hadn't noticed it before. It is definitely time for an awareness session.

Perhaps you could coordinate this with a cell phone notification or the ringing of church bells at a local church. You can even make this a habit when you make your coffee in the morning.

3. Mindful Drinking

Yes, you may have already experienced mindful eating, but you can extend this to the drinking of certain liquids. Imagine becoming totally absorbed in the drinking of the first cup of coffee or tea in the morning. As a coffee drinker, I find this a naturally mindful moment.

I create a mindful event out of drinking coffee at the beginning of every day. I start with my favorite flavor of my favorite brand, then I grind the beans and inhale the amazing aroma. Then let the brewing begin. But my mindfulness of the process hasn't stopped. As I become fully engaged with the aroma of the coffee brewing, I'm aware of its presence and my feelings about it. Then, as I pour the coffee, I watch as it flows from the pot to the cup. I notice the shape the flow takes and the nuances of color.

As I cup my hands around the mug, I become fully engaged in the coffee's taste, warmth and my sensations surrounding this morning ritual. Yes, that's a mindful approach to drinking coffee. What's your favorite beverage? Can you bring a similar approach to drinking it?

4. View Everything as Interesting

It may be easy to see how a pink rose or a baby could be interesting. But challenge yourself by viewing an annoying interruption as interesting. Instead of getting upset, step back from yourself and observe what's happening. Watch as your mind reacts to this. What type of sensations do you feel? As these well up inside of you, carefully pay attention to them.

This is a great exercise to keep a small incident from exploding into a large issue. In effect, you can do what some of the wisest individuals do: laugh it off. That may be a difficult reaction at first, but you will at least develop the ability to view it at a distance. That, in itself, will help you.

This exercise can also be a vital tool in helping you realize the importance of being in the present moment. If you can view even events which are annoying as interesting, you're well on the way to mindful living.

5. Care About Your Work

This is another tip that sounds absurd to some of us. Your first response may very well be: "I don't care about my work." Therein lies the challenge. Choose one portion of your day that you can begin to initially view as just "interesting," and then learn to like it. While you're tempted to say lunch or break in jest, don't laugh. If that's all you can muster at first, so be it. At least it's a start.

As soon as you can begin a mindful approach to even this small part of your work day, you'll eventually find that more and more of your day unfolds in an interesting fashion. Eventually, while you're wrapped in awareness, you'll find more aspects of your job to like. Start with finding something – anything – about your job as interesting. Let it blossom from there.

6. Practice the Fine Art of Gratitude

Indeed, being thankful for people and things in your life is really nothing more than being fully aware of how they affect your life. You're bringing a mindful awareness to the people who mean the most to you, examining what they've done for you and then thanking them for this. Indeed, it's a simple use of mindfulness that can transform your life.

7. The Red Light of Mindfulness

In the previous chapter, we talked about how driving – particularly your commute to work

– can be a call to mindfulness. If you believe that an entire mindful commute is too much of a challenge (and on some days it really is!), select one aspect of driving to use as a trigger to gently enter the state of mindfulness.

One of the most practical ways: a stop light. A red light just might be the perfect length of time to allow you to draw in several breaths and to become fully aware of your surroundings as well as your own physical body. Drain yourself of any lingering negative emotions that may have crept up while you've been driving. Most of us have a few stop lights we encounter. These are perfect intervals to "de-stress" from the rat race to work.

Once the light changes to green, begin driving again. If you can, try to salvage some of that mindfulness. Savor as much of the present moment as you can until you reach the next traffic signal. You know what to do when you get stopped at the next one. Once you begin doing this, you'll be hoping to catch those lights red!

8. Stop! Even Before You Open that Door.

As you reach for the door when you leave for work each day, pause. This informal mindfulness reminder takes a mere 30 seconds of your time. Re-posture yourself. Stand with your shoulders back. Straighten your back. For this short time, gain an awareness of your physical body.

Bring your awareness to bear on your feet. Observe how they feel as they touch the floor. If during this short time the mind is pressing you to think about something else, gently bring your attention back to your feet. Once approximately 30 seconds has passed, continue on with your day. You'll discover you're much more grounded.

9. Approach Your Communications with Mindfulness.

You might think of this suggestion as *Mission Impossible*. Of course, it's going to be if you view it like that. Before you dismiss this, consider the immeasurable consequences it may have in your life. Whether you're doing the talking or you're listening, enter the communication process with a mindful approach. Initially, you'll find you can only remember to do this once or twice during the day, but as you find the treasure in this approach, it'll become a habit.

If you're talking, become aware of the sound of your own voice – the inflections, the tone, the volume. Anything and everything about your speech. If the other person is speaking, totally absorb yourself in their voice, inflections, and even the body language of the other person. You know what to do should your mind start to wander. Bring it back to the present conversation, without judging yourself. In this way, you'll not only be practicing mindfulness, but you're also developing extremely effective communication skills.

10. Fulfill Your Thirst for Knowledge.

You may not even know you're thirsty for knowledge. Why not enter a mindful state through reading, studying a new subject, or even developing a new skill? The act of learning something new requires your presence in the moment. It's hard to read a book and try to absorb the material without paying attention to the present. You'll discover you're not only stretching your horizons, but expanding your ability to live in the present.

Conclusion: "Who Knows? We'll See!"

At the start of your study of mindfulness, we talked about entering your meditation with a beginner's mind, open to all possibilities. Right about now, you realize the importance of that mind. It's only while you're in this state that you can fully become aware of the present moment. It's only from this state that you can step back, suspend judgment, and watch your life play out much like a movie.

When you can approach even snatches of your life like the Japanese farmer in the story below, then you can truly appreciate being mindful. The following story is a vivid illustration of the value of everything we've just discussed. Watch how life unfolds for this farmer who suspends judgment on the events of his life.

A Man and His Horse

A farmer had one horse. Now this horse was not in the healthiest of shape, but it had been with the farmer for a long time. Having compassion for this animal, the man allowed the horse to go free. He let him loose to spend his last years in the nearby mountains.

This act of compassion horrified his neighbors, who wondered how the farmer would earn a living without his horse. "What terrible luck you have," they informed him. The farmer nodded, then quietly spoke these words, "Who knows? We'll see."

Not more than a week had passed when the horse returned – much healthier. Not only that, but the now-healthy horse brought an entourage of nearly a half dozen younger horses with him. Now, this farmer who just recently had no horses had a stable of horses. "What great luck," his neighbors said, excited for the change of his fortune. But the farmer reacted in his customary, calm way, "Who knows?" he said, "We'll see."

It wasn't long before the farmer's son approached the horses in order to break and train the new ones. In the process, he broke his leg. Once again, the neighbors gathered around him to extend their sincere sympathy. "How can you farm now without the help of your able-bodied son?" they asked. "How terribly unfortunate," they lamented. Again, the enigmatic farmer merely shook his head and gave them his now standard answer. "Who knows? We'll see."

It didn't take long for the farmer and the rest of the village to see. Several days later, the Emperor's army came through the village, forcing all of the young and able men into conscription. As it turned out, the farmer's son was not conscripted into service. He was deemed unable to fight because of his broken leg. "Why, that's wonderful!" the townspeople exclaimed. "How lucky you are!" This time, the farmer allowed just the hint of a smile to cross his lips. He shook his head slightly and said: "Who knows? We'll see."

In some versions of this ancient story, this is where it ends. But there is another version that adds this final episode:

The leg of the farmer's son didn't heal quite properly so he walked with a limp. The neighbors yet again gathered around to pay their sympathy to the family. "What a shame," they said, "that's some bad luck you've run into again." And yes, once again the old wise farmer merely smiled and said, "Who knows? We'll see."

The war which the farmer's son couldn't fight in finally ended. It seemed that the vast majority of the able-bodied young men who went off to war didn't return. They were killed in battle. This left only the farmer and his son to work the majority of the area land. As a result, they became very rich.

Now the neighbors once again gathered around and just shook their heads at the incredible good fortune of the family. "You must have been born under a lucky star," one friend commented. "What tremendous luck you have!" Do I need tell you how the farmer responded to this? This farmer knew how to cultivate and keep a beginner's mind.

Goals. We All Need Goals.

Not all of us can hold on to such a mindset as this farmer did. But now that you know there is another view of your life out there – beyond judgment and open to many possibilities – you can begin developing your own beginner's mind.

It's now your turn to reply to friends when they begin to judge the events of your life: "Who knows? We'll see." Even more importantly, the moment your mind jumps to judgmental conclusions you can stop it with the same words: "Who knows? We'll see."

Appendix: Basic Instructions for a Mindful Sitting Meditation

The following set of instructions provides you the basics of a mindful sitting meditation. This simple act can be adjusted again and again whether you're lying down, walking, or sitting cross-legged to suit your personal needs. Keep in mind the pose may change, but the process stays the same.

1. Sit in a chair.

As I said in the introduction to this appendix, you certainly may adjust these instructions so you can lie down, sit in a full-lotus position, or any other position you choose.

As you sit, though, get comfortable. This may mean, like Goldilocks, trying out several different chairs. Your legs should be touching the floor comfortably. You don't want your knees to be bent too far nor do you want to have to stretch your legs to reach the floor.

2. Close your eyes.

Some individuals meditate with their eyes open. In time, you may want to do this. But as you begin, try meditating with your eyes closed. This helps you to focus better, keeping distractions to a minimum.

3. Put your hands on your lap.

Again, as you develop this practice and make it your own, you may find a more comfortable location for your hands. But this is the most common pose: hands on lap with palms up. Some persons find that using a "mudra" aids their concentration. This is a special placement of the hands which helps you to remember you're in meditation. One of the most common of these is the classic thumb touching the forefinger.

4. Center yourself.

Relax your entire body. This may seem obvious, but you'll be surprised at how many individuals realize in the middle of their meditation that some of portion of their body is still tense. I'm definitely one of them.

5. Place your focus on the abdomen.

You don't need to look at the lower abdomen, but you do want to move a hand from your lap to this area. This will help you stay focused and develop the mindful awareness necessary for this meditation.

6. Observe and feel the rising and falling of your breath.

When you breathe in you'll notice your abdomen naturally expands. When you exhale, your abdomen contracts. Observe this rhythmic action. Place your awareness to this process for ten full breaths. During this time your mind should be totally focused on your breath and abdomen. You may find your mind wanders even for this short period of time. If it does, gently bring it back to being aware of your breath.

7. Take another 10.

After you can keep your mind on your breath for the initial count of ten, try it for a second set. All the while, keep your hand on your abdomen.

8. Observe the process from a detached perspective.

This is, without a doubt, one of the most difficult of the guidelines to understand, let alone follow. Try to feel the movement of your abdomen as if it were occurring to someone else. Think of the times you've dreamt of being the main character in your dreams. You know the action is happening to you but at the same time you're watching it as if it were happening to another person.

9. Stay in the present moment.

This is the most important part of any meditation program. If you've been observing your breath, this should be a natural extension of this activity. Of course, when you discover you're straddling either side of the fence – the past or the future – bring yourself squarely to the present and your breath.

10. Label the moment.

This step is often misunderstood by many. To label something doesn't mean to judge it. It's neither good nor bad, right nor wrong. Labeling means identifying it for what it is. When you're labeling your breaths, you'll call one rising and the other falling.

That's all there is to a mindfulness meditation. As you continue with this practice, you'll be able to add more onto it. You'll be following the awareness of your body as well as your surroundings.

Also By Jennifer Brooks

The Four Day Meditation Solution - Use the Power of Meditation to Transform Your Life from Ordinary to Extraordinary ... In Just Four Days

Meditation, Not Medication - Heal Yourself Using Your Mind-Body Connection with Healing Meditation

Zen Meditation Magic: Secrets to Finding the Time for Peace of Mind, Everyday

Related Books You Will Enjoy

How to Quiet Your Mind (Bestseller): Relax and Silence the Voice of Your Mind Today to Reduce Stress and Achieve Inner Peace Using Meditation! - A Beginner's Guide – Marc Allen

Your Perfect Life - How to Use the Law of Attraction to Get the Life You Deserve – Susan Edwards

The Stress Free You: How to Live Stress Free and Feel Great Everyday, Starting Today – Elizabeth O'Brien

Visit EmpowermentNation.com to view these books and more!

Visit
EmpowermentNation.com
to view other fantastic books,
sign up for book alerts, giveaways, and
updates!

Printed in Great Britain
by Amazon.co.uk, Ltd.,
Marston Gate.